Table of Contents

Chocolate rice cakes 3
Bounty Bars 5
Butter Cookies 7
Confetti cake in a mug 9
Teriyaki chicken bites 11
Sticky chicken bites 13
Berry blast smoothie 15
Strawberry Smoothie 17
Malibu Sunset 19
Vanilla ice cream 21

THE SNACKERS.

ISBN: 978-1-0370-0697-5

Chocolate rice cakes

Ingredients

>1 packet rice cakes
>handful of chopped almonds/peanuts
>1 cup melted milk chocolate
>shredded coconut

Method

>On the stove over high heat, place a small pot with water and bring to a boil.
>Place a small bowl over the boiling water with the chocolate until the chocolate is fully melted.
>Remove from stove.
>Dip the rice cakes in the chocolate and sprinkle them with the nuts and a little bit of the coconut.

Bounty Bars

Ingredients

>1 cup shredded coconut
>1/2 cup sweetened condensed milk
>1 cup melted milk chocolate

Method

>In a small bowl pour in the condensed milk and the shredded coconut.
>Mix until well combined.
>Scoop and shape into small balls.
>Dip each ball in the melted chocolate and let sit in the fridge for about 30 minutes.
>Repeat the process until all the balls are coated in chocolate.

Butter Cookies

Ingredients

>1 stick of butter (1/2 cup)
>1/2 cup white granulated sugar
>1 egg
>1 tsp vanilla extract
>2 cups AP flour
>1 tbsp baking powder

Method

>Pre-heat oven to 180
>In a bowl, add in the stick of butter and place in the microwave until melted.
>In the same bowl add in the sugar, egg and vanilla extract. Mix until well combined.
>In a separate bowl add in the dry ingredients and mix. Proceed to add the wet ingredients to the dry ones.
>Mix well until the dough forms a very soft dough
>Scoop and shape into balls
>Place the balls on a baking tray lined with parchment paper and gently press on them with a fork.
>Place in the microwave for 10-15 minutes or until golden brown.

Confetti cake in a mug

Ingredients

>2 ½ cups AP flour
>1 cup milk
>1/3 cup butter
>1/2 cup sugar
>1 tsp vanilla extract
>2 tsp baking powder
>1 egg
>1 tsp oil
>1/3 cup hot water

Method

>In a bowl combine the flour, baking powder and the confetti sprinkles.
>Make a well in the middle and add the milk, butter, sugar and vanilla extract.
>Mix until well combined.
>Pour the batter equally in six standard mugs
>Microwave for one and a half minutes on high
>Take out of the microwave and sprinkle a little bit of powdered sugar
>Enjoy!

Teriyaki chicken bites

Ingredients

>6 chicken thighs
>1/3 cup soy sauce
>1/3 cup brown sugar
>1 tbsp cooking oil

Method

>Wash and cut the chicken into cubes
>In a large frying pan, heat the oil over medium heat
>Add in the chicken and fry for about 5 minutes or until cooked through
>Add in the soy sauce followed by the sugar. Mix and stir until the sauce thickens
>Remove from heat
>Serve with a side of cilantro rice
>Enjoy!

Sticky chicken bites

Ingredients

>4 chicken breasts
>2 tbsp oil
>1/3 cup honey
>1/3 cup soy sauce
>1 clove of garlic, minced
>salt and pepper to taste

Method

>In a small bowl combine the honey, soy sauce, garlic and the salt and pepper to form a sauce
>In a pan over medium heat, toss the chicken until golden brown
>Add the sauce and simmer until the sauce thickens
>Remove from stove
>Serve and enjoy

Berry blast smoothie

Ingredients

>1 cup frozen strawberries
>1 cup frozen blueberries
>1/2 cup plain yoghurt
>1 tsp honey
>1/2 cup milk of choice

Method

>In a blender start by pouring in the liquids followed by the frozen berries
>Blend until smooth and creamy

Berry blast smoothie

Strawberry Smoothie

Ingredients

>1 cup frozen strawberries
>1 banana
>1 cup milk of choice

Method

>Mix everything in the blender until smooth
>Serve and enjoy.

Malibu Sunset

Ingredients

>1/2 cup cranberry juice
>1 cup sprite lemon-lime flavoured drink
>1/2 cup orange juice
>1 cup ice cubes

Method

>In a glass, start by pouring in the ice cubes followed by the cranberry juice, the sprite then the orange juice
>Garnish with a slice of orange or mint leave

Vanilla ice cream

Ingredients

>1/2 cup condensed milk
>1 cup heavy cream/ whipping cream

Method

>In a large bowl, pour in the whipping cream and whip until stiff peaks form
>Add in the condensed milk and gently mix until fully combined
>Transfer the ice cream in a freezer safe bowl with a lid
>Place in the freezer for a minimum of 4 hours or overnight to set.
>Serve with a slice of chocolate cake
>Enjoy!

www.ingramcontent.com/pod-product-compliance
Lightning Source LLC
Chambersburg PA
CBHW040753020526
44118CB00042B/2933